GW01406543

Cram101 Textbook Outlines to accompany:

Cognitive Psychology: Mind and Brain

Smith & Kosslyn, 1st Edition

A Cram101 Inc. publication (c) 2009.

Cram101 Textbook Outlines and Cram101.com are Cram101 Inc. publications and services. All notes, highlights, reviews, and practice tests are written and prepared by Cram101, all rights reserved.

PRACTICE EXAMS.

Get all of the self-teaching practice exams for each chapter of this textbook at **www.Cram101.com** and ace the tests. Here is an example:

Chapter 1

Cognitive Psychology: Mind and Brain
Smith & Kosslyn, 1st Edition,
All Material Written and Prepared by Cram101

I WANT A BETTER GRADE.   Items 1 - 50 of 100. ▶

1 A _____ is a final product of a specific mental/cognitive process by an individual or group, which is called _____ making, or in more detail, Inactive _____ making, Reactive _____ making, and Proactive _____ making.

  ◯ Decision   ◯ Dactylozooid
  ◯ Daddy longleg   ◯ D-amino acid oxidase activator

2 _____ is the cognitive process leading to the selection of a course of action among variations. Every _____ process produces a final choice. It can be an action or an opinion. It begins when we need to do something but know not what. Therefore, _____ is a reasoning process which can be rational or irrational, and can be based on explicit assumptions or tacit assumptions.

  ◯ Decision making   ◯ Dactylozooid
  ◯ Daddy longleg   ◯ D-amino acid oxidase activator

3 _____, in its most general definition, is a complex psychophysical process that arises spontaneously, rather than through conscious effort, and evokes either a positive or negative psychological response and physical expressions, often involuntary, related to feelings, perceptions or beliefs about elements, objects or relations between them, in reality or in the imagination. An _____ is often differentiated from a feeling.

  ◯ Emotion   ◯ Eagle
  ◯ Ear   ◯ Eardrum

4 A _____ is an obstacle which makes it difficult to achieve a desired goal, objective or purpose. It refers to a

You get a 50% discount for the online exams. Go to **Cram101.com**, click Sign Up at the top of the screen, and enter DK73DW4082 in the promo code box on the registration screen. Access to Cram101.com is $4.95 per month, cancel at any time.

With Cram101.com online, you also have access to extensive reference material.

You will nail those essays and papers. Here is an example from a Cram101 Biology text:

Visit **www.Cram101.com**, click Sign Up at the top of the screen, and enter DK73DW4082 in the promo code box on the registration screen. Access to www.Cram101.com is normally $9.95 per month, but because you have purchased this book, your access fee is only $4.95 per month, cancel at any time. Sign up and stop highlighting textbooks forever.

Learning System

Cram101 Textbook Outlines is a learning system. The notes in this book are the highlights of your textbook, you will never have to highlight a book again.

How to use this book. Take this book to class, it is your notebook for the lecture. The notes and highlights on the left hand side of the pages follow the outline and order of the textbook. All you have to do is follow along while your intructor presents the lecture. Circle the items emphasized in class and add other important information on the right side. With Cram101 Textbook Outlines you'll spend less time writing and more time listening. Learning becomes more efficient.

Cram101.com Online

Increase your studying efficiency by using Cram101.com's practice tests and online reference material. It is the perfect complement to Cram101 Textbook Outlines. Use self-teaching matching tests or simulate in-class testing with comprehensive multiple choice tests, or simply use Cram's true and false tests for quick review. Cram101.com even allows you to enter your in-class notes for an integrated studying format combining the textbook notes with your class notes.

Visit **www.Cram101.com**, click Sign Up at the top of the screen, and enter **DK73DW4082** in the promo code box on the registration screen. Access to www.Cram101.com is normally $9.95, but because you have purchased this book, your access fee is only $4.95. Sign up and stop highlighting textbooks forever.

Copyright © 2009 by Cram101, Inc. All rights reserved. "Cram101"® and "Never Highlight a Book Again!"® are registered trademarks of Cram101, Inc. ISBN(s): 1-4288-5972-1, 9781428859722 .

Cognitive Psychology: Mind and Brain
Smith & Kosslyn, 1st

CONTENTS

Decision	A decision is a final product of a specific mental/cognitive process by an individual or group, which is called decision making, or in more detail, Inactive decision making, Reactive decision making, and Proactive decision making.
Decision making	Decision making is the cognitive process leading to the selection of a course of action among variations. Every decision making process produces a final choice. It can be an action or an opinion. It begins when we need to do something but know not what. Therefore, decision making is a reasoning process which can be rational or irrational, and can be based on explicit assumptions or tacit assumptions.
Emotion	Emotion, in its most general definition, is a complex psychophysical process that arises spontaneously, rather than through conscious effort, and evokes either a positive or negative psychological response and physical expressions, often involuntary, related to feelings, perceptions or beliefs about elements, objects or relations between them, in reality or in the imagination. An emotion is often differentiated from a feeling.
Problem	A problem is an obstacle which makes it difficult to achieve a desired goal, objective or purpose. It refers to a situation, condition, or issue that is yet unresolved.
Problem solving	Problem solving forms part of thinking. Considered the most complex of all intellectual functions, problem solving has been defined as higher-order cognitive process that requires the modulation and control of more routine or fundamental skills.
Cognition	In psychology, cognition refers to an information processing view of an individual's psychological functions. Other interpretations of the meaning of cognition link it to the development of concepts; individual minds, groups, organizations, and even larger coalitions of entities, can be modelled as societies which cooperate to form concepts.
Cognitive psychology	Cognitive psychology is the school of psychology that examines internal mental processes such as problem solving, memory, and language.
Psychology	Psychology is both an academic and applied discipline involving the scientific study of mental processes and behavior. Psychology is one of the behavioral sciences a broad field that spans the social and natural sciences. Psychology attempts to understand the role human behavior plays in social dynamics while incorporating physiological and neurological processes into its conceptions of mental functioning.
Consciousness	The awareness of the sensations, thoughts, and feelings being experienced at a given moment is called consciousness.
Behaviorism	Behaviorism is a philosophy of psychology based on the proposition that all things which organisms do including acting, thinking and feeling can and should be regarded as behaviors. Behaviorism comprises the position that all theories should have observational correlates but that there are no philosophical differences between publicly observable processes and privately observable processes.
Functionalism	Functionalism was created by William James and influenced by Darwin. This school of psychology focuses on past experience and behavior. It adressed how experience permits people to function better in our environment. According to functionalism, the mental states that make up consciousness can essentially be defined as complex interactions between different functional processes.
Psychologist	A psychologist is a scientist or clinician who studies psychology, the systematic investigation of the human mind, including behavior and cognition. Psychologist is usually categorized under a number of different fields.
Mechanism	In philosophy, mechanism is a theory that all natural phenomena can be explained by physical causes. It can be contrasted with vitalism, the philosophical theory that vital forces are active in living organisms, so that life cannot be explained solely by mechanism.
Computer	A computer is a machine which manipulates data according to a list of instructions which makes it an

Go to **Cram101.com** for the Practice Tests for this Chapter.
And, **NEVER** highlight a book again!

ideal example of a data processing system.

Mind	Mind collectively refers to the aspects of intellect and consciousness manifested as combinations of thought, perception, memory, emotion, will and imagination; mind is the stream of consciousness.
Dendrite	A dendrite is one of the numerous branched projections of a neuron that act to conduct the electrical stimulation received from other neural cells to the cell body, or soma, of the neuron from which the dendrites project. Dendrites play a critical role in integrating these synaptic inputs and in determining the extent to which action potentials are produced by the neuron.
Synapse	A synapse is specialized junction through which cells of the nervous system signal to one another and to non-neuronal cells such as muscles or glands. They allow the neurons of the central nervous system to form interconnected neural circuits.
Neuron	The neuron is the primary cell of the nervous system. They are found in the brain, the spinal cord, in the nerves and ganglia of the peripheral nervous system. It is a specialized cell that conducts impulses through the nervous system and contains three major parts: cell body, dendrites, and an axon. It can have many dendrites but only one axon.
Central nervous system	The central nervous system represents the largest part of the nervous system, including the brain and the spinal cord. Together with the peripheral nervous system, it has a fundamental role in the control of behavior. The CNS is contained within the dorsal cavity, with the brain within the cranial subcavity, and the spinal cord in the spinal cavity. The CNS is covered by the meninges. The brain is also protected by the skull, and the spinal cord is also protected by the vertebrae.
Nervous system	The nervous system of an animal coordinates the activity of the muscles, monitors the organs, constructs and also stops input from the senses, and initiates actions.
Nervous system autonomic	Nervous system autonomic is the part of the peripheral nervous system that acts as a control system, maintaining homeostasis in the body.
Action potential	An action potential is a "spike" of electrical discharge that travels along the membrane of a cell.
Structure	Structure is a fundamental and sometimes intangible notion covering the recognition, observation, nature, and stability of patterns and relationships of entities.
Cerebral cortex	The cerebral cortex is a structure within the vertebrate brain with distinct structural and functional properties.
Fight-or-flight response	The fight-or-flight response was first described by Walter Cannon; this theory states that animals react to threats with a general discharge of the sympathetic nervous system, priming the animal for fighting or fleeing.
Parasympathetic nervous system	The parasympathetic nervous system is a division of the autonomic nervous system, along with the sympathetic nervous system and Enteric nervous system. The ANS is a subdivision of the peripheral nervous system.
Sympathetic nervous system	The Sympathetic nervous system is a branch of the autonomic nervous system. It is always active at a basal level and becomes more active during times of stress. Its actions during the stress response comprise the fight-or-flight response. The sympathetic nervous system is responsible for up- and down-regulating many homeostatic mechanisms in living organisms.
Cortex	In anatomy and zoology the cortex is the outermost layer of an organ. Organs with well-defined cortical layers include kidneys, adrenal glands, ovaries, the thymus, and portions of the brain, including the cerebral cortex, the most well-know of all cortices.
Role	A role is a set of connected behaviors, rights and obligations as conceptualized by actors in a social situation. It is mostly defined as an expected behavior in a given individual social status and social position.
Occipital lobe	The occipital lobe is the visual processing center of the mammalian brain, containing most of the

Go to **Cram101.com** for the Practice Tests for this Chapter.
And, **NEVER** highlight a book again!

anatomical region of the visual cortex. The primary visual cortex is Brodmann area 17, commonly called V_1.

Parietal lobe

The parietal lobe is a lobe in the brain. It is positioned above the occipital lobe and behind the frontal lobe.

Function

The mathematical concept of a function expresses dependence between two quantities, one of which is given the independent variable, argument of the function, or its "input" and the other produced the dependent variable, value of the function, or "output".

Temporal lobe

The temporal lobe is part of the cerebrum. It lies at the side of the brain, beneath the lateral or Sylvian fissure. Adjacent areas in the superior, posterior and lateral parts of the temporal lobe are involved in high-level auditory processing.

Broca face=symbol>-s area

Broca's area is a section of the human brain that is involved in language processing, speech production and comprehension.

Frontal lobe

The frontal lobe comprises four major folds of cortical tissue: the precentral gyrus, superior gyrus and the middle gyrus of the frontal gyri, the inferior frontal gyrus. It has been found to play a part in impulse control, judgement, language, memory, motor function, problem solving, sexual behavior, socialization and spontaneity.

Primary motor cortex

The primary motor cortex works in association with pre-motor areas to plan and execute movements. It contains large neurons known as Betz cells which send long axons down the spinal cord to synapse onto alpha motor neurons which connect to the muscles.

Thalamus

An area near the center of the brain involved in the relay of sensory information to the cortex and in the functions of sleep and attention is the thalamus.

Motor cortex

Motor cortex is a term that describes regions of the cerebral cortex involved in the planning, control, and execution of voluntary motor functions.

Brain

In animals, the brain, is the control center of the central nervous system, responsible for behavior. The brain is located in the head, protected by the skull and close to the primary sensory apparatus of vision, hearing, equilibrioception, sense of acceleration, taste, and olfaction.

Hippocampus

The hippocampus is a part of the brain located in the medial temporal lobe. It forms a part of the limbic system and plays a part in memory and spatial navigation.

Hypothalamus

The hypothalamus is a region of the brain located below the thalamus, forming the major portion of the ventral region of the diencephalon and functioning to regulate certain metabolic processes and other autonomic activities.

Limbic system

The limbic system includes the putative structures in the human brain involved in emotion, motivation, and emotional association with memory. The limbic system influences the formation of memory by integrating emotional states with stored memories of physical sensations.

Amygdala

Amygdala are almond-shaped groups of neurons located deep within the medial temporal lobes of the brain in complex vertebrates, including humans. Shown in research to perform a primary role in the processing and memory of emotional reactions, the amygdala are considered part of the limbic system.

Cerebellum

The cerebellum is a region of the brain that plays an important role in the integration of sensory perception and motor output. Many neural pathways link the cerebellum with the motor cortex—which sends
information to the muscles causing them to move—and the spinocerebellar tract—which provides feedback on the position of the body in space. The cerebellum integrates these pathways, using the constant feedback on body position to fine-tune motor movements.

Reticular formation

The reticular formation is a part of the brain which is involved in stereotypical actions, such as walking, sleeping, and lying down. It is essential for governing some of the basic functions of higher

Go to **Cram101.com** for the Practice Tests for this Chapter.
And, **NEVER** highlight a book again!

organisms, and phylogenetically one of the oldest portions of the brain.

Intelligence	Intelligence is a property of mind that encompasses many related abilities, such as the capacities to reason, plan, solve problems, think abstractly, comprehend ideas and language, and learn. In some cases intelligence may include traits such as creativity, personality, character, knowledge, or wisdom. However other psychologists prefer not to include these traits in the definition of intelligence.
Study skills	Study skills are strategies and methods of purposeful learning, usually centered around reading and writing. Effective study skills are considered essential for students to acquire good grades in school, and are useful in general to improve learning throughout one's life, in support of career and other interests.
Cognitive neuroscience	Cognitive neuroscience is an academic field concerned with the scientific study of biological mechanisms underlying cognition, with a specific focus on the neural substrates of mental processes and their behavioral manifestations. It addresses the questions of how psychological/cognitive functions are produced by the neural circuitry.
Dissociation	Dissociation is a state of acute mental decompensation in which certain thoughts, emotions, sensations, and/or memories are compartmentalized because they are too overwhelming for the conscious mind to integrate. This subconscious strategy for managing powerful negative emotions is sometimes referred to as "splitting", as these thoughts, emotions, sensations, and/or memories are "split off" from the integrated ego.
Judgment	A judgment is synonymous with the formal decision made by a court following a lawsuit. At the same time the court may also make a range of court orders, such as imposing a sentence upon a guilty defendant in a criminal matter, or providing a remedy for the plaintiff in a civil law matter.
Protocol	In the natural sciences, a protocol is a predefined written procedural method in the design and implementation of experiments. This should establish standards that can be adequately assessed by peer review and provide for successful replication of results by others in the field.
Floor effect	In statistics, the term floor effect refers to when data cannot take on a value lower than some particular number, called the floor.
Event-related potential	An event-related potential is any stereotyped electrophysiological response to an internal or external stimulus. More simply, it is any measured brain response that is directly the result of a thought or perception.
Functional magnetic resonance imaging	Functional magnetic resonance imaging is the use of MRI to measure the haemodynamic response related to neural activity in the brain or spinal cord of humans or other animals. It is one of the most recently developed forms of neuroimaging.
Magnetic resonance imaging	Magnetic resonance imaging is a non-invasive method used to render images of the inside of an object. It is primarily used in medical imaging to demonstrate pathological or other physiological alterations of living tissues.
Positron emission tomography	Positron emission tomography is a nuclear medicine medical imaging technique which produces a three-dimensional image or map of functional processes in the body. Images of metabolic activity in space are then reconstructed by computer, often in modern scanners aided by results from a CT X-ray scan.
Electroencep-alography	Electroencephalography is the measurement of electrical activity produced by the brain as recorded from electrodes placed on the scalp.
PET	A pet is an animal kept for companionship and enjoyment, as opposed to livestock, laboratory animals, working animals or sport animals, which are kept for economic reasons.
Neuropsychol-gical	Neuropsychological test is specifically designed task used to measure a psychological function known to be linked to a particular brain structure or pathway. Most are based on traditional psychometric theory. It usually involves the systematic administration of clearly defined procedures in a formal

Go to Cram101.com for the Practice Tests for this Chapter.

	environment.
Experiment	In the scientific method, an experiment is a set of observations performed in the context of solving a particular problem or question, to support or falsify a hypothesis or research concerning phenomena. The experiment is a cornerstone in the empirical approach to acquiring deeper knowledge about the physical world.
Transcranial magnetic stimulation	A Transcranial magnetic stimulation is a noninvasive method to excite neurons in the brain.
Stimulation	Stimulation is the action of various agents on muscles, nerves, or a sensory end organ, by which activity is evoked.
Paradox	A paradox can be an apparently true statement or group of statements that leads to a contradiction or a situation which defies intuition; or it can be, seemingly opposite, an apparent contradiction that actually expresses a non-dual truth.

Go to **Cram101.com** for the Practice Tests for this Chapter.
And, **NEVER** highlight a book again!

Perception	In psychology. and the cognitive sciences, perception is the process of acquiring, interpreting, selecting, and organizing sensory information. It is a task far more complex than was imagined in the 1950s and 1960s, when it was proclaimed that building perceiving
Cognition	In psychology, cognition refers to an information processing view of an individual's psychological functions. Other interpretations of the meaning of cognition link it to the development of concepts; individual minds, groups, organizations, and even larger coalitions of entities, can be modelled as societies which cooperate to form concepts.
Problem	A problem is an obstacle which makes it difficult to achieve a desired goal, objective or purpose. It refers to a situation, condition, or issue that is yet unresolved.
Visual perception	In psychology, visual perception is the ability to interpret visible light information reaching the eyes which is then made available for planning and action.
Structure	Structure is a fundamental and sometimes intangible notion covering the recognition, observation, nature, and stability of patterns and relationships of entities.
Bottom-up	If your attention is drawn to a flower in a field, it may be simply that the flower is more visually salient than the surrounding field. The information which caused you to attend to the flower came to you in a bottom-up fashion -- your attention was not contingent upon knowledge of the flower; the outside stimulus was sufficient on its own.
Bottom-up process	In perception theory, a bottom-up process is a mental procedure that brings the features of the individual stimulus recorded by the senses together to form a perception of larger objects or scenery.
Top-down	Top-down processing is the observation that person's perception and recognition of objects is influenced by the physical and mental context in which the objects are encountered.
Learning	Learning is the acquisition and development of memories and behaviors, including skills, knowledge, understanding, values, and wisdom. It is the goal of education, and the product of experience. Learning ranges from simple forms such as habituation to more complex forms such as play, seen only in large vertebrates.
Ganglion	In anatomy, a ganglion is a tissue mass.
Acne	Acne Vulgaris is a skin disease, caused by changes in the pilosebaceous units. Severe acne is inflammatory, but acne can also manifest in noninflammatory forms.
Illusion	An illusion is a distortion of a sensory perception, revealing how the brain normally organizes and interprets sensory stimulation. While illusions distort reality, they are generally shared by most people. Illusions may occur with more of the human senses than vision, but visual illusions, optical illusions, are the most well known and understood.
Operant conditioning	Operant conditioning is the use of consequences to modify the occurrence and form of behavior. It deals with the modification of "voluntary behavior" through the use of consequences. According to the laws of operant conditioning, any behavior that is consistently rewarded, every single time, will extinguish at a faster rate while intermittently reinforcing behavior leads to more stable rates of behavior that are
Optic chiasm	The optic chiasm is the part of the brain where the optic nerves partially cross. Specifically, the nerves connected to the right eye that attend to the left visual field cross with the nerves from the left eye that attend to the right visual field.
Conditioning	Conditioning is a form of associative learning that was first demonstrated by Ivan Pavlov. The typical procedure for inducing classical conditioning involves presentations of a neutral stimulus along with a stimulus of some significance. The neutral stimulus could be any event that does not result in an overt behavioral response from the organism under investigation.

Go to **Cram101.com** for the Practice Tests for this Chapter.
And, **NEVER** highlight a book again!

Cortex	In anatomy and zoology the cortex is the outermost layer of an organ. Organs with well-defined cortical layers include kidneys, adrenal glands, ovaries, the thymus, and portions of the brain, including the cerebral cortex, the most well-know of all cortices.
Cortical column	A cortical column is a group of neurons in the brain cortex which can be successively penetrated by a probe inserted perpendicularly to the cortical surface, and which have nearly identical receptive fields.
Organizing	Organizing is the act of rearranging elements following one or more rules. It can also be seen as the opposite of messing up. One organized opposite could be disordered, since ordered is almost synonymous. The difference between ordered and organized is that something is only ordered as long as it is both organized and standardized.
Population	In sociology and biology a population is the collection of people or individuals of a particular species. A population shares a particular characteristic of interest most often that of living in a given geographic area.
Color vision	Color vision is the capacity of an organism or machine to distinguish objects based on the wavelengths of the light they reflect or emit. The nervous system derives color by comparing the responses to light from the several types of cone photoreceptors in the eye.
Uniform	A uniform is a set of standard clothing worn by members of an organization while participating in that organization's activity.
Connectedness	Connectedness is a psychological term used to describe the quality and number of connections we have with other people in our social circle of family, friends and acquaintances. The more socially connected a person is in their lives, generally the greater sense of self-control and self-determination they feel.
Proxemics	The term proxemics was introduced by anthropologist Edward T. Hall in 1959 to describe set measurable distances between people as they interact.
Similarity	Similarity refers to the psychological nearness or proximity of two mental representations. In social psychology, similarity refers to how closely attitudes, values, interests and personality match between people. Research has consistently shown that similarity leads to interpersonal attraction.
Illusory contours	Illusory contours are a form of visual illusion where contours are perceived without a luminance or color change across the contour. Friedrich Schumann discovered illusory contours.
Binding problem	The binding problem is "the problem of how the unity of conscious perception is brought about by the distributed activities of the central nervous system." It arises whenever information from distinct populations of neurons must be combined. The activity of specialised sets of neurons dealing with different aspects of perception are combined to form a unified perceptual experience.
Recognition	Recognition is a process that occurs in thinking when some event, process, pattern, or object recurs. Thus in order for something to be recognized, it must be familiar. In philosophy recognition became very important in Hegel's attempt at understanding the emergence of self-consciousness.
Brain	In animals, the brain, is the control center of the central nervous system, responsible for behavior. The brain is located in the head, protected by the skull and close to the primary sensory apparatus of vision, hearing, equilibrioception, sense of acceleration, taste, and olfaction.
Entity	An entity is something that has a distinct, separate existence, though it need not be a material existence. In particular, abstractions and legal fictions are usually regarded as an

Go to **Cram101.com** for the Practice Tests for this Chapter.
And, **NEVER** highlight a book again!

	entity. In general, there is also no presumption that an entity is animate.
Geon	A geon is a simple 3-dimensional form such as a sphere, cube, cylinder, cone or wedge. One often-cited theory of object recognition, Biederman's recognition-by-componentstheory, proposes that visual input is matched against structural representations of objects in the brain.
Face perception	Face perception is the process by which the brain and mind understand and interpret the face, particularly the human face.
Priming	Priming in psychology refers to activating parts of particular representations or associations in memory just before carrying out an action or task. It is considered to be one of the manifestations of implicit memory. A property of priming is that the remembered item is remembered best in the form in which it was originally encountered. If a priming list is given in an auditory mode, then an auditory cue produces better performance than a visual
Expert	An expert is someone widely recognized as a reliable source of technique or skill whose faculty for judging or deciding rightly, justly, or wisely is accorded authority and status by their peers or the public. An expert, more generally, is a person with extensive knowledge or ability in a particular area of study.
Hypothesis	A hypothesis consists either of a suggested explanation for a phenomenon or of a reasoned proposal suggesting a possible correlation between multiple phenomena.
Brightness	Brightness is an attribute of visual perception in which a source appears to emit a given amount of light. In other words, brightness is the perception elicited by the luminance of a visual target. This is a subjective attribute/property of an object being observed.
Context effect	The context effect is an effect where cognition and memory are dependent on context, such that out-of-context memories are more difficult to retrieve than in-context memories.
Hermann Ebbinghaus	Hermann Ebbinghaus was a German psychologist who pioneered experimental study of memory, and discovered the forgetting curve and the learning curve. His famous work on memory helped to initiate experimental psychology. He pioneered precise experimental techniques used in the research on learning.
Feedback	In organizational context, feedback is a process of sharing observations, concerns and suggestions with the other person with an intention of improving his/her performance as an individual. Feedback has to be bi-directional so that continuous improvement is possible in an organization.
Modelling	Modelling in psychology is a method used in certain techniques of psychotherapy whereby the client learns by imitation alone or a general process in which persons serve as models for others.
Neural network	A neural network describes a population of physically interconnected neurons or a group of disparate neurons whose inputs or signalling targets define a recognizable circuit. Communication between neurons often involves an electrochemical process.
Adaptation	An adaptation is a positive characteristic of an organism that has been favored by natural selection. The concept is central to biology, particularly in evolutionary biology. The term adaptation is also sometimes used as a synonym for natural selection, but most biologists discourage this usage.
Competition	Competition is the rivalry of two or more parties over something. Competition occurs naturally between living organisms which coexist in an environment with limited resources
Visual processing	Visual processing is the sequence of steps that information takes as it flows from visual sensors to cognitive processing. The sensors may be zoological eyes or they may be cameras or sensor arrays that sense various portions of the electromagnetic spectrum.

Go to **Cram101.com** for the Practice Tests for this Chapter.

Go to **Cram101.com** for the Practice Tests for this Chapter.
And, **NEVER** highlight a book again!

Dopamine	Dopamine is a hormone and neurotransmitter occurring in a wide variety of animals, including both vertebrates and invertebrates. In the brain, dopamine functions as a neurotransmitter. Dopamine is also a neurohormone released by the hypothalamus. Its main function as a hormone is to inhibit the release of prolactin from the anterior lobe of the pituitary.

18

Go to **Cram101.com** for the Practice Tests for this Chapter.

Go to **Cram101.com** for the Practice Tests for this Chapter.
And, **NEVER** highlight a book again!

Attention	Attention is the cognitive process of selectively concentrating on one aspect of the environment while ignoring other things. Examples include listening carefully to what someone is saying while ignoring other conversations in the room or listening to a cell phone
Role	A role is a set of connected behaviors, rights and obligations as conceptualized by actors in a social situation. It is mostly defined as an expected behavior in a given individual social status and social position.
Change blindness	In visual perception, change blindness is the phenomenon where a person viewing a visual scene apparently fails to detect large changes in the scene. For change blindness to occur, the change in the scene typically has to coincide with some visual, disruption such as a saccade (eye movement) or a brief obscuration of the observed scene or image.
Blindness	Blindness is the condition of lacking visual perception due to physiological or neurological factors.
Hearing impairment	A hearing impairment is a full or partial decrease in the ability to detect or understand sounds.[1] Caused by a wide range of biological and environmental factors, loss of hearing can happen to any organism that perceives sound.
Space	The idea of space has been of interest for philosophers and scientists for much of human history. The term is used somewhat differently in different fields of study, hence it is difficult to provide an uncontroversial and clear definition outside of specific defined contexts. Disagreement also exists on whether space itself can be measured or is part of the measuring system.
Top-down	Top-down processing is the observation that person's perception and recognition of objects is influenced by the physical and mental context in which the objects are encountered.
Attentional blink	Attentional blink is a phenomenon observed in rapid serial visual presentation (RSVP). When presented with a sequence of visual stimuli in rapid succession at the same spatial location on a screen, a participant will often fail to detect a second salient target occurring in succession if it is presented between 200-500ms after the first one.
Problem	A problem is an obstacle which makes it difficult to achieve a desired goal, objective or purpose. It refers to a situation, condition, or issue that is yet unresolved.
Hemispatial neglect	Hemispatial neglect is a neurological condition in which, after damage to one hemisphere of the brain, a deficit in attention to the opposite side of space is observed.
Neglect	Neglect means to leave uncared for or to leave undone.
Endogenous	An emotion or behavior is endogenous if it is spontaneously generated from an individual's internal state.
Exogenous	Exogenous refers to an action or object coming from outside a system. In attentional psychology, exogenous refers to attention being drawn without conscious intention. An example of this would be attention drawn to a flashing light in the periphery of vision.
Mind	Mind collectively refers to the aspects of intellect and consciousness manifested as combinations of thought, perception, memory, emotion, will and imagination; mind is the stream of consciousness.
Priming	Priming in psychology refers to activating parts of particular representations or associations in memory just before carrying out an action or task. It is considered to be one of the manifestations of implicit memory. A property of priming is that the remembered item is remembered best in the form in which it was originally encountered. If a priming list is given in an auditory mode, then an auditory cue produces better performance than a visual
Experiment	In the scientific method, an experiment is a set of observations performed in the context of

Go to **Cram101.com** for the Practice Tests for this Chapter.
And, **NEVER** highlight a book again!

solving a particular problem or question, to support or falsify a hypothesis or research concerning phenomena. The experiment is a cornerstone in the empirical approach to acquiring deeper knowledge about the physical world.

Functional magnetic resonance imaging

Functional magnetic resonance imaging is the use of MRI to measure the haemodynamic response related to neural activity in the brain or spinal cord of humans or other animals. It is one of the most recently developed forms of neuroimaging.

Brain

In animals, the brain, is the control center of the central nervous system, responsible for behavior. The brain is located in the head, protected by the skull and close to the primary sensory apparatus of vision, hearing, equilibrioception, sense of acceleration, taste, and olfaction.

Brain damage

Brain damage is the destruction or degeneration of brain cells. It may occur due to a wide range of conditions, illnesses, injuries, and as a result of iatrogenesis. Possible causes of widespread brain damage include prolonged hypoxia, poisoning by teratogens, infection, and neurological illness.

Syndrome

The term syndrome is the association of several clinically recognizable features, signs, symptoms, phenomena or characteristics which often occur together, so that the presence of one feature indicates the presence of the others.

Agnosia

Agnosia is a loss of ability to recognize objects, persons, sounds, shapes, or smells while the specific sense is not defective nor is there any significant memory loss. It is usually associated with brain injury or neurological illness, particularly after damage to the temporal lobe.

Dichotic listening

In cognitive psychology, dichotic listening is a procedure commonly used to investigate selective attention in the auditory system. In dichotic listening, two different auditory stimuli are presented to the participant simultaneously, one to each ear, normally using a set of headphones. Participants are asked to attend to one or both of the messages. They may later be asked about the content of either message.

Theory

In common usage, people often use the word theory to signify a conjecture, an opinion, or a speculation. In this usage, a theory is not necessarily based on facts; in other words, it is not required to be consistent with true descriptions of reality.

Feature integration theory

The feature integration theory, developed by Treisman and Gelade since the early 1980s has been one of the most influential psychological models of human visual attention. According to Treisman, in a first step to visual processing, several primary visual features are processed and represented with separate feature maps that are later integrated in a saliency map that can be accessed in order to direct attention to the most conspicuous areas.

Event-related potential

An event-related potential is any stereotyped electrophysiological response to an internal or external stimulus. More simply, it is any measured brain response that is directly the result of a thought or perception.

Electrophysi-logy

Electrophysiology is the study of the electrical properties of biological cells and tissues. It involves measurements of voltage change or electrical current flow on a wide variety of scales from single ion channel proteins to whole tissues like the heart.

PET

A pet is an animal kept for companionship and enjoyment, as opposed to livestock, laboratory animals, working animals or sport animals, which are kept for economic reasons.

Monitoring

Monitoring generally means to be aware of the state of a system.

Cortex

In anatomy and zoology the cortex is the outermost layer of an organ. Organs with well-defined cortical layers include kidneys, adrenal glands, ovaries, the thymus, and portions of

Go to **Cram101.com** for the Practice Tests for this Chapter.
And, **NEVER** highlight a book again!

the brain, including the cerebral cortex, the most well-know of all cortices.

Competition	Competition is the rivalry of two or more parties over something. Competition occurs naturally between living organisms which coexist in an environment with limited resources

Go to **Cram101.com** for the Practice Tests for this Chapter.
And, **NEVER** highlight a book again!

Long-term memory	Long-term memory is memory, stored as meaning, that can last as little as 30 seconds or as long as decades. It differs structurally and functionally from working memory or short-term memory, which ostensibly stores items for only around 30 seconds.
Knowledge	Knowledge is defined variously as expertise, and skills acquired by a person through experience or education; the theoretical or practical understanding of a subject, what is known in a particular field or in total; facts and information or awareness or familiarity gained by experience of a fact or situation.
Memory	In psychology, memory is an organism's ability to store, retain, and subsequently retrieve information. In recent decades, it has become one of the principal pillars of a branch of science called cognitive neuroscience, an interdisciplinary link between cognitive psychology and neuroscience.
Cognition	In psychology, cognition refers to an information processing view of an individual's psychological functions. Other interpretations of the meaning of cognition link it to the development of concepts; individual minds, groups, organizations, and even larger coalitions of entities, can be modelled as societies which cooperate to form concepts.
Role	A role is a set of connected behaviors, rights and obligations as conceptualized by actors in a social situation. It is mostly defined as an expected behavior in a given individual social status and social position.
Categorization	Categorization is the process in which ideas and objects are recognized, differentiated and understood.
Animal language	Animal language is the modeling of human language in non human animal systems.
Inference	Inference is the act or process of drawing a conclusion based solely on what one already knows.
Language	A language is a system of symbols and the rules used to manipulate them. Language can also refer to the use of such systems as a general phenomenon. Though commonly used as a means of communication among people, human language is only one instance of this phenomenon.
Understanding	Understanding is a psychological process related to an abstract or physical object, such as, person, situation, or message whereby one is able to think about it and use concepts to deal adequately with that object.
Mind	Mind collectively refers to the aspects of intellect and consciousness manifested as combinations of thought, perception, memory, emotion, will and imagination; mind is the stream of consciousness.
Criterion	A criterion is a condition/rule which enables a choice, therefore upon which a decision or judgment can be based.
Brain	In animals, the brain, is the control center of the central nervous system, responsible for behavior. The brain is located in the head, protected by the skull and close to the primary sensory apparatus of vision, hearing, equilibrioception, sense of acceleration, taste, and olfaction.
Attention	Attention is the cognitive process of selectively concentrating on one aspect of the environment while ignoring other things. Examples include listening carefully to what someone is saying while ignoring other conversations in the room or listening to a cell phone conversation while driving a car.
Behavior	Behavior refers to the actions or reactions of an object or organism, usually in relation to the environment. Behavior can be conscious or unconscious, overt or covert, and voluntary or involuntary.

Go to **Cram101.com** for the Practice Tests for this Chapter.

Go to **Cram101.com** for the Practice Tests for this Chapter.
And, **NEVER** highlight a book again!

Interference theory	Interference theory refers to the idea that forgetting occurs because the recall of certain items interferes with the recall of other items. In nature, the interfering items are said to originate from an overstimulating environment. This theory along with the decay theory have been proposed as reasons for why people forget. Evidence for this theory comes from paired associate learning.
Working memory	Working memory is a theoretical framework within cognitive psychology that refers to the structures and processes used for temporarily storing and manipulating information. There are numerous theories as to both the theoretical structure of working memory as well as to the specific parts of the brain responsible for working memory.
Neuron	The neuron is the primary cell of the nervous system. They are found in the brain, the spinal cord, in the nerves and ganglia of the peripheral nervous system. It is a specialized cell that conducts impulses through the nervous system and contains three major parts: cell body, dendrites, and an axon. It can have many dendrites but only one axon.
Visual processing	Visual processing is the sequence of steps that information takes as it flows from visual sensors to cognitive processing. The sensors may be zoological eyes or they may be cameras or sensor arrays that sense various portions of the electromagnetic spectrum.
Pattern	A pattern, from the French patron meaning model, is a theme of reoccurring events or objects, sometimes referred to as elements of a set. These elements repeat in a predictable manner. It can be a template or model which can be used to generate things or parts of a thing, especially if the things that are created have enough in common for the underlying pattern to be inferred, in which case the things are said to exhibit the pattern.
Perception	In psychology. and the cognitive sciences, perception is the process of acquiring, interpreting, selecting, and organizing sensory information. It is a task far more complex than was imagined in the 1950s and 1960s, when it was proclaimed that building perceiving machines would take about a decade, but, needless to say, that is still very far from reality.
Power	Much of the recent sociological debate on power revolves around the issue of the enabling nature of power.
Mechanism	In philosophy, mechanism is a theory that all natural phenomena can be explained by physical causes. It can be contrasted with vitalism, the philosophical theory that vital forces are active in living organisms, so that life cannot be explained solely by mechanism.
Functional magnetic resonance imaging	Functional magnetic resonance imaging is the use of MRI to measure the haemodynamic response related to neural activity in the brain or spinal cord of humans or other animals. It is one of the most recently developed forms of neuroimaging.
PET	A pet is an animal kept for companionship and enjoyment, as opposed to livestock, laboratory animals, working animals or sport animals, which are kept for economic reasons.
Positron emission tomography	Positron emission tomography is a nuclear medicine medical imaging technique which produces a three-dimensional image or map of functional processes in the body. Images of metabolic activity in space are then reconstructed by computer, often in modern scanners aided by results from a CT X-ray scan.
Neuroimaging	Neuroimaging includes the use of various techniques to either directly or indirectly image the structure, function/pharmacology of the brain. It is a relatively new discipline within medicine and neuroscience.
Structure	Structure is a fundamental and sometimes intangible notion covering the recognition, observation, nature, and stability of patterns and relationships of entities.

Go to **Cram101.com** for the Practice Tests for this Chapter.
And, **NEVER** highlight a book again!

Association	Association is a widely used memory tool. In psychology and marketing, two concepts or stimuli are associated when the experience of one leads to the effects of another, due to repeated pairing.
Entity	An entity is something that has a distinct, separate existence, though it need not be a material existence. In particular, abstractions and legal fictions are usually regarded as an entity. In general, there is also no presumption that an entity is animate.
Temporal lobe	The temporal lobe is part of the cerebrum. It lies at the side of the brain, beneath the lateral or Sylvian fissure. Adjacent areas in the superior, posterior and lateral parts of the temporal lobe are involved in high-level auditory processing.
Association areas	Association areas are areas of the brain that do not constitute the somatosensory, motor, auditory or visual cortices. The association areas comprise of about 75% of the cerebral cortex and are believed to link the sensory and motor cortices.
Shape	Shape, refers to the external two-dimensional outline, appearance or configuration of some thing — in contrast to the matter or content or substance of which it is composed.

Go to **Cram101.com** for the Practice Tests for this Chapter.
And, **NEVER** highlight a book again!

Encoding	Encoding (in cognition) is a basic perceptual process of interpreting incoming stimuli; technically speaking, it is a complex, multi-stage process of converting relatively objective sensory input (e.g., light, sound) into subjectively meaningful experience.
Episodic memory	Episodic memory refers to the memory of events, times, places, associated emotions, and other conception-based knowledge in relation to an experience. Semantic and episodic memory together make up the category of declarative memory, which is one of the two major divisions in memory.
Long-term memory	Long-term memory is memory, stored as meaning, that can last as little as 30 seconds or as long as decades. It differs structurally and functionally from working memory or short-term memory, which ostensibly stores items for only around 30 seconds.
Memory	In psychology, memory is an organism's ability to store, retain, and subsequently retrieve information. In recent decades, it has become one of the principal pillars of a branch of science called cognitive neuroscience, an interdisciplinary link between cognitive psychology and neuroscience.
Organizing	Organizing is the act of rearranging elements following one or more rules. It can also be seen as the opposite of messing up. One organized opposite could be disordered, since ordered is almost synonymous. The difference between ordered and organized is that something is only ordered as long as it is both organized and standardized.
Explicit memory	Explicit memory is the conscious, intentional recollection of previous experiences and information.
Semantic memory	Semantic memory refers to the memory of meanings, understandings, and other concept-based knowledge unrelated to specific experiences.
Power	Much of the recent sociological debate on power revolves around the issue of the enabling nature of power.
Temporal lobe	The temporal lobe is part of the cerebrum. It lies at the side of the brain, beneath the lateral or Sylvian fissure. Adjacent areas in the superior, posterior and lateral parts of the temporal lobe are involved in high-level auditory processing.
Structure	Structure is a fundamental and sometimes intangible notion covering the recognition, observation, nature, and stability of patterns and relationships of entities.
Working memory	Working memory is a theoretical framework within cognitive psychology that refers to the structures and processes used for temporarily storing and manipulating information. There are numerous theories as to both the theoretical structure of working memory as well as to the specific parts of the brain responsible for working memory.
Surgery	In medicine, surgery is the medical specialty that treats diseases or injuries by operative manual and instrumental treatment.
Priming	Priming in psychology refers to activating parts of particular representations or associations in memory just before carrying out an action or task. It is considered to be one of the manifestations of implicit memory. A property of priming is that the remembered item is remembered best in the form in which it was originally encountered. If a priming list is given in an auditory mode, then an auditory cue produces better performance than a visual
Attention	Attention is the cognitive process of selectively concentrating on one aspect of the environment while ignoring other things. Examples include listening carefully to what someone is saying while ignoring other conversations in the room or listening to a cell phone conversation while driving a car.
Theory	In common usage, people often use the word theory to signify a conjecture, an opinion, or a speculation. In this usage, a theory is not necessarily based on facts; in other words, it is

Go to **Cram101.com** for the Practice Tests for this Chapter.
And, **NEVER** highlight a book again!

	not required to be consistent with true descriptions of reality.
Generation	Generation, also known as procreation, is the act of producing offspring. A generation can also be a stage or degree in a succession of natural descent as a grandfather, a father, and the father's son comprise three generations.
Experiment	In the scientific method, an experiment is a set of observations performed in the context of solving a particular problem or question, to support or falsify a hypothesis or research concerning phenomena. The experiment is a cornerstone in the empirical approach to acquiring deeper knowledge about the physical world.
Practice	Most commonly, practice is a learning method, the act of rehearsing a behavior over and over, or engaging in an activity again and again, for the purpose of improving or mastering it, as in the phrase "practice makes perfect".
Recollection	Recollection is the retrieval of memory. It is not a passive process; people employ metacognitive strategies to make the best use of their memory, and priming and other context can have a large effect on what is retrieved.
Pattern	A pattern, from the French patron meaning model, is a theme of reoccurring events or objects, sometimes referred to as elements of a set. These elements repeat in a predictable manner. It can be a template or model which can be used to generate things or parts of a thing, especially if the things that are created have enough in common for the underlying pattern to be inferred, in which case the things are said to exhibit the pattern.
Source amnesia	Source amnesia is an explicit memory disorder in which someone can recall certain information, but do not know where or how it was obtained. As source amnesia prohibits recollection of the context specific information surrounding facts in experienced events, there is also the inclusive case of confusion concerning the content or context of events, a highly attributable factor to confabulation in brain disease.
Amnesia	Amnesia is a condition in which memory is disturbed. The causes of amnesia are organic or functional. Organic causes include damage to the brain, through trauma or disease, or use of certain generally sedative drugs.
Frontal lobe	The frontal lobe comprises four major folds of cortical tissue: the precentral gyrus, superior gyrus and the middle gyrus of the frontal gyri, the inferior frontal gyrus. It has been found to play a part in impulse control, judgement, language, memory, motor function, problem solving, sexual behavior, socialization and spontaneity.
Function	The mathematical concept of a function expresses dependence between two quantities, one of which is given the independent variable, argument of the function, or its "input" and the other produced the dependent variable, value of the function, or "output".
Bias	A bias is a prejudice in a general or specific sense, usually in the sense for having a preference to one particular point of view or ideological perspective.
Measurement	Measurement is the estimation of the magnitude of some attribute of an object, such as its length or weight, relative to a unit of measurement. Measurement usually involves using an instrument, such as a ruler or scale, which is calibrated to compare the object to some standard, such as a meter or a kilogram.
Recognition	Recognition is a process that occurs in thinking when some event, process, pattern, or object recurs. Thus in order for something to be recognized, it must be familiar. In philosophy recognition became very important in Hegel's attempt at understanding the emergence of self-consciousness.
Forgetting	Forgetting is a spontaneous or gradual process in which old memories are unable to be recalled from memory storage. It is subject to delicately balanced optimization that ensures

Go to **Cram101.com** for the Practice Tests for this Chapter.
And, **NEVER** highlight a book again!

that relevant memories are recalled.

Interference theory	Interference theory refers to the idea that forgetting occurs because the recall of certain items interferes with the recall of other items. In nature, the interfering items are said to originate from an overstimulating environment. This theory along with the decay theory have been proposed as reasons for why people forget. Evidence for this theory comes from paired associate learning.
Proactive	In behavioral medicine, proactive often refers to a treatment approach where a therapist initiates contacts as opposed to reactive where the responsibility for contacts with the therapist is entirely on the client e.g. proactive and reactive quitlines for tobacco or alcohol.
Competition	Competition is the rivalry of two or more parties over something. Competition occurs naturally between living organisms which coexist in an environment with limited resources
Association	Association is a widely used memory tool. In psychology and marketing, two concepts or stimuli are associated when the experience of one leads to the effects of another, due to repeated pairing.
Mechanism	In philosophy, mechanism is a theory that all natural phenomena can be explained by physical causes. It can be contrasted with vitalism, the philosophical theory that vital forces are active in living organisms, so that life cannot be explained solely by mechanism.
Vocabulary	The vocabulary of a person is defined either as the set of all words that are understood by that person or the set of all words likely to be used by that person when constructing new sentences. Even though the two words are synonymous, "curse" is a regular part of the vocabulary of most native English speakers while "imprecate" is not.
Brain	In animals, the brain, is the control center of the central nervous system, responsible for behavior. The brain is located in the head, protected by the skull and close to the primary sensory apparatus of vision, hearing, equilibrioception, sense of acceleration, taste, and olfaction.
Brain damage	Brain damage is the destruction or degeneration of brain cells. It may occur due to a wide range of conditions, illnesses, injuries, and as a result of iatrogenesis. Possible causes of widespread brain damage include prolonged hypoxia, poisoning by teratogens, infection, and neurological illness.
Neuroimaging	Neuroimaging includes the use of various techniques to either directly or indirectly image the structure, function/pharmacology of the brain. It is a relatively new discipline within medicine and neuroscience.
Observation	Observation is an activity of a sapient or sentient living being, which senses and assimilates the knowledge of a phenomenon in its framework of previous knowledge and ideas.
Skill learning	Skill learning is the gradual retainment of new abilities and functions such as cognitive motor and perceptual skills.
Learning	Learning is the acquisition and development of memories and behaviors, including skills, knowledge, understanding, values, and wisdom. It is the goal of education, and the product of experience. Learning ranges from simple forms such as habituation to more complex forms such as play, seen only in large vertebrates.
Habit	An habit is an automatic routine of behavior that are repeated regularly, without thinking. They are learned, not instinctive, human behaviors that occur automatically, without the explicit contemporaneous intention of the person. The person may not be paying attention to or be conscious or aware of the behavior.

Go to **Cram101.com** for the Practice Tests for this Chapter.
And, **NEVER** highlight a book again!

Computer	A computer is a machine which manipulates data according to a list of instructions which makes it an ideal example of a data processing system.
Memory	In psychology, memory is an organism's ability to store, retain, and subsequently retrieve information. In recent decades, it has become one of the principal pillars of a branch of science called cognitive neuroscience, an interdisciplinary link between cognitive psychology
Experiment	In the scientific method, an experiment is a set of observations performed in the context of solving a particular problem or question, to support or falsify a hypothesis or research concerning phenomena. The experiment is a cornerstone in the empirical approach to acquiring deeper knowledge about the physical world.
Duration	A duration is an amount of time or a particular time interval.
Sensory memory	Sensory memory is the ability to retain impressions of sensory information after the original stimulus has ceased. It refers to items detected by the sensory receptors which are retained temporarily in the sensory registers and which have a large capacity for unprocessed information but are only able to hold accurate images of sensory information momentarily.
Recollection	Recollection is the retrieval of memory. It is not a passive process; people employ metacognitive strategies to make the best use of their memory, and priming and other context can have a large effect on what is retrieved.
Accessibility	Accessibility is a general term used to describe the degree to which a product is accessible by as many people as possible. Accessibility can also be viewed as the "ability to access" the functionality, and possible benefit, of some system or entity; such a definition brings in access-based individual rights laws and regulations.
Understanding	Understanding is a psychological process related to an abstract or physical object, such as, person, situation, or message whereby one is able to think about it and use concepts to deal adequately with that object.
Comprehension	The comprehension of an object is the totality of intensions, that is, attributes, characters, marks, properties, or qualities, that the object possesses, or else the totality of intensions that are pertinent to the context of a given discussion. This is the correct technical term for the whole collection of intensions of an object.
Neuroimaging	Neuroimaging includes the use of various techniques to either directly or indirectly image the structure, function/pharmacology of the brain. It is a relatively new discipline within medicine and neuroscience.
Information processing	Information processing is the change of information in any manner detectable by an observer. As such, it is a process which describes everything which happens in the universe, from the falling of a rock to the printing of a text file from a digital computer system.
Function	The mathematical concept of a function expresses dependence between two quantities, one of which is given the independent variable, argument of the function, or its "input" and the other produced the dependent variable, value of the function, or "output".
Organizing	Organizing is the act of rearranging elements following one or more rules. It can also be seen as the opposite of messing up. One organized opposite could be disordered, since ordered is almost synonymous. The difference between ordered and organized is that something is only ordered as long as it is both organized and standardized.
Independence	Independence is the self-government of a nation, country, or state by its residents and population, or some portion thereof, generally exercising sovereignty.
Short-term memory	Short-term memory is that part of memory which is said to be able to hold a small amount of information for about 20 seconds. The information held in short-term memory may be: recently processed sensory input; items recently retrieved from long-term memory; or the result of

Go to **Cram101.com** for the Practice Tests for this Chapter.
And, **NEVER** highlight a book again!

recent mental processing, although that is more generally related to the concept of working memory.

Mechanism	In philosophy, mechanism is a theory that all natural phenomena can be explained by physical causes. It can be contrasted with vitalism, the philosophical theory that vital forces are active in living organisms, so that life cannot be explained solely by mechanism.
Mnemonic	A mnemonic is an aid for memory . They rely not only on repetition to remember facts, but also on associations between easy-to-remember constructs and lists of data, based on the principle that the human mind much more easily remembers insignificant data attached to spatial, personal, or otherwise meaningful information than that occurring in meaningless sequences.
Working memory	Working memory is a theoretical framework within cognitive psychology that refers to the structures and processes used for temporarily storing and manipulating information. There are numerous theories as to both the theoretical structure of working memory as well as to the specific parts of the brain responsible for working memory.
Cortex	In anatomy and zoology the cortex is the outermost layer of an organ. Organs with well-defined cortical layers include kidneys, adrenal glands, ovaries, the thymus, and portions of the brain, including the cerebral cortex, the most well-know of all cortices.
Prefrontal cortex	The prefrontal cortex is the anterior part of the frontal lobes of the brain, lying in front of the motor and premotor areas. Cytoarchitectonically, it is defined by the presence of an internal granular layer IV.
Role	A role is a set of connected behaviors, rights and obligations as conceptualized by actors in a social situation. It is mostly defined as an expected behavior in a given individual social status and social position.
Brain	In animals, the brain, is the control center of the central nervous system, responsible for behavior. The brain is located in the head, protected by the skull and close to the primary sensory apparatus of vision, hearing, equilibrioception, sense of acceleration, taste, and olfaction.
Monkey	A monkey is the third group being the apes. There are 264 known extant species of monkey. It ranges in size t 14-16 cm and 120-140 g in weight. Some are arboreal, some live on the savannah; diets differ among the various species but may contain any of the following: fruit, leaves, seeds, nuts, flowers, insects, spiders, eggs and small animals.
Theory	In common usage, people often use the word theory to signify a conjecture, an opinion, or a speculation. In this usage, a theory is not necessarily based on facts; in other words, it is not required to be consistent with true descriptions of reality.
Episodic buffer	Baddeley extended the model of working memory by adding a fourth component, the episodic buffer, which holds representations that integrate phonological, visual, and spatial information, and possibly information not covered by the slave systems.
Dopamine	Dopamine is a hormone and neurotransmitter occurring in a wide variety of animals, including both vertebrates and invertebrates. In the brain, dopamine functions as a neurotransmitter. Dopamine is also a neurohormone released by the hypothalamus. Its main function as a hormone is to inhibit the release of prolactin from the anterior lobe of the pituitary.

Go to **Cram101.com** for the Practice Tests for this Chapter.
And, **NEVER** highlight a book again!

Frontal lobe	The frontal lobe comprises four major folds of cortical tissue: the precentral gyrus, superior gyrus and the middle gyrus of the frontal gyri, the inferior frontal gyrus. It has been found to play a part in impulse control, judgement, language, memory, motor function,
Syndrome	The term syndrome is the association of several clinically recognizable features, signs, symptoms, phenomena or characteristics which often occur together, so that the presence of one feature indicates the presence of the others.
Wisconsin Card Sorting Test	The Wisconsin Card Sorting Test is a neuropsychological test of "set-shifting", i.e. the ability to display flexibility in the face of changing schedules of reinforcement.
Tower of Hanoi	The Tower of Hanoi is a mathematical game or puzzle. It consists of three pegs, and a number of disks of different sizes which can slide onto any peg. The puzzle starts with the disks neatly stacked in order of size on one peg, the smallest at the top, thus making a conical shape.
Alzheimer face=symbol>-s	Alzheimer's disease is a neurodegenerative disease that, in its most common form, is found in people over age 65. Clinical signs of Alzheimer's disease are characterized by progressive cognitive deterioration, together with declining activities of daily living and by neuropsychiatric symptoms or behavioral changes. It is the most common type of dementia.
Disease	A disease is an abnormal condition of an organism that impairs bodily functions. In human beings, "disease" is often used more broadly to refer to any condition that causes discomfort, dysfunction, distress, social problems, and/or death to the person afflicted, or similar problems for those in contact with the person.
Dysfunction	Dysfunction in psychology is an abnormality.
Attention	Attention is the cognitive process of selectively concentrating on one aspect of the environment while ignoring other things. Examples include listening carefully to what someone is saying while ignoring other conversations in the room or listening to a cell phone conversation while driving a car.
Conflict	Conflict is a state of discord caused by the actual or perceived opposition of needs, values and interests between people.
Neuroimaging	Neuroimaging includes the use of various techniques to either directly or indirectly image the structure, function/pharmacology of the brain. It is a relatively new discipline within medicine and neuroscience.
Categorization	Categorization is the process in which ideas and objects are recognized, differentiated and understood.
Consciousness	The awareness of the sensations, thoughts, and feelings being experienced at a given moment is called consciousness.
Role	A role is a set of connected behaviors, rights and obligations as conceptualized by actors in a social situation. It is mostly defined as an expected behavior in a given individual social status and social position.
Trial	In law, a trial is an event in which parties to a dispute present information in a formal setting, usually a court, before a judge, jury, or other designated finder of fact, in order to achieve a resolution to their dispute.
Information processing	Information processing is the change of information in any manner detectable by an observer. As such, it is a process which describes everything which happens in the universe, from the falling of a rock to the printing of a text file from a digital computer system.
Hypothesis	A hypothesis consists either of a suggested explanation for a phenomenon or of a reasoned proposal suggesting a possible correlation between multiple phenomena.

Go to **Cram101.com** for the Practice Tests for this Chapter.

Go to **Cram101.com** for the Practice Tests for this Chapter.
And, **NEVER** highlight a book again!

Meta-analysis	In statistics, a meta-analysis combines the results of several studies that address a set of related research hypotheses. The first meta-analysis was performed by Karl Pearson in 1904, in an attempt to overcome the problem of reduced statistical power in studies with small sample sizes; analyzing the results from a group of studies can allow more accurate data analysis.
Experiment	In the scientific method, an experiment is a set of observations performed in the context of solving a particular problem or question, to support or falsify a hypothesis or research concerning phenomena. The experiment is a cornerstone in the empirical approach to acquiring deeper knowledge about the physical world.
Mechanism	In philosophy, mechanism is a theory that all natural phenomena can be explained by physical causes. It can be contrasted with vitalism, the philosophical theory that vital forces are active in living organisms, so that life cannot be explained solely by mechanism.
Association	Association is a widely used memory tool. In psychology and marketing, two concepts or stimuli are associated when the experience of one leads to the effects of another, due to repeated pairing.
Monitoring	Monitoring generally means to be aware of the state of a system.
Memory	In psychology, memory is an organism's ability to store, retain, and subsequently retrieve information. In recent decades, it has become one of the principal pillars of a branch of science called cognitive neuroscience, an interdisciplinary link between cognitive psychology and neuroscience.
Working memory	Working memory is a theoretical framework within cognitive psychology that refers to the structures and processes used for temporarily storing and manipulating information. There are numerous theories as to both the theoretical structure of working memory as well as to the specific parts of the brain responsible for working memory.
Number	A number is an abstract idea used in counting and measuring. A symbol which represents a number is called a numeral, but in common usage the word number is used for both the idea and the symbol. In addition to their use in counting and measuring, numerals are often used for labels, for ordering, and for codes.

Go to **Cram101.com** for the Practice Tests for this Chapter.
And, **NEVER** highlight a book again!

Cognition	In psychology, cognition refers to an information processing view of an individual's psychological functions. Other interpretations of the meaning of cognition link it to the development of concepts; individual minds, groups, organizations, and even larger coalitions
Emotion	Emotion, in its most general definition, is a complex psychophysical process that arises spontaneously, rather than through conscious effort, and evokes either a positive or negative psychological response and physical expressions, often involuntary, related to feelings, perceptions or beliefs about elements, objects or relations between them, in reality or in the imagination. An emotion is often differentiated from a feeling.
Brain	In animals, the brain, is the control center of the central nervous system, responsible for behavior. The brain is located in the head, protected by the skull and close to the primary sensory apparatus of vision, hearing, equilibrioception, sense of acceleration, taste, and olfaction.
Amygdala	Amygdala are almond-shaped groups of neurons located deep within the medial temporal lobes of the brain in complex vertebrates, including humans. Shown in research to perform a primary role in the processing and memory of emotional reactions, the amygdala are considered part of the limbic system.
Anger	Anger is a an emotion. It is a psychophysiological response to pain, perceived suffering or distress, or threat thereof, which has been uncalled for or unjustly brought upon oneself or others, at least from a subjective viewpoint. A threat may be real, discussed, or imagined.
Disgust	Disgust is an emotion that is typically associated with things that are perceived as unclean, inedible, or infectious. Disgust is one of the basic emotions of Robert Plutchik's theory of emotions. Disgust invokes a characteristic facial expression, one of Paul Ekman's six universal facial expressions of emotion.
Fear	Fear is an emotional response to tangible and realistic dangers. Fear should be distinguished from anxiety, an emotion that often arises out of proportion to the actual threat or danger involved, and can be subjectively experienced without any specific attention to the threatening object.
Happiness	Happiness is an emotional or affective state that is characterized by feelings of enjoyment, pleasure, and satisfaction. As a state and a subject, it has been pursued and commented on extensively throughout world history.
Sadness	Sadness is a mood that displays feeling of disadvantage and loss. Deep immersion in this feeling may lead eventually to depression a pathological state, which may require intervention by a qualified professional. Usually while in a state of sadness, the person becomes quiet, less energetic and withdraws into oneself.
Surprise	Surprise is a brief emotional state that is the result of experiencing an unexpected event. Surprise can have any valence, that is, they can be neutral, pleasant, or unpleasant. Accordingly, some would not categorize surprise in itself as an emotion.
Interpersonal Circumplex	The interpersonal circumplex is a model for conceptualizing, organizing, and assessing interpersonal behavior, traits, and motives. The interpersonal circumplex is defined by two orthogonal axes: a vertical axis and a horizontal axis. In recent years, it has become conventional to identify the vertical and horizontal axes with the broad constructs of agency and communion. Thus, each point in the interpersonal circumplex space can be specified as a weighted combination of agency and communion.
Cortex	In anatomy and zoology the cortex is the outermost layer of an organ. Organs with well-defined cortical layers include kidneys, adrenal glands, ovaries, the thymus, and portions of the brain, including the cerebral cortex, the most well-know of all cortices.
Motivation	Motivation is a reason or set of reasons for engaging in a particular behavior, especially

Go to **Cram101.com** for the Practice Tests for this Chapter.

Go to **Cram101.com** for the Practice Tests for this Chapter.
And, **NEVER** highlight a book again!

human behavior as studied in psychology and neuropsychology. The reasons may include basic needs e.g., food, water, shelter or an object, goal, state of being, or ideal that is desirable, which may or may not be viewed as "positive," such as seeking a state of being in which pain is absent. The motivation for a behavior may also be attributed to less-apparent reasons such as altruism or morality.

Withdrawal	Withdrawal, also known as withdrawal syndrome, refers to the characteristic signs and symptoms that appear when a drug that causes physical dependence is regularly used for a long time and then suddenly discontinued or decreased in dosage.
Mood	A mood is a relatively lasting emotional or affective state. They differ from emotions in that they are less specific, often less intense, less likely to be triggered by a particular stimulus or event, however longer lasting.
Assessment	Assessment is the process of documenting, usually in measurable terms, knowledge, skills, attitudes and beliefs. An assessment can be classified in many different ways. The most important distinctions are: (1) formative and summative; (2) objective and subjective; (3) referencing (criterion-referenced, norm-referenced, and ipsative); and (4) informal and formal.
Induction	Induction is a method of artificially or prematurely stimulating labor in a woman.
Measurement	Measurement is the estimation of the magnitude of some attribute of an object, such as its length or weight, relative to a unit of measurement. Measurement usually involves using an instrument, such as a ruler or scale, which is calibrated to compare the object to some standard, such as a meter or a kilogram.
Autonomic nervous system	The autonomic nervous system is the part of theperipheral nervous system that acts as a control system, maintaining homeostasis in the body. These maintenance activities are primarily performed without conscious control or sensation. . Its most useful definition could be: the sensory and motor neurons that innervate the viscera. These neurons form reflex arcs that pass through the lower brainstem or medulla oblongata.
Skin	In zootomy and dermatology, skin is the largest organ of the integumentary system made up of multiple layers of epithelial tissues that guard underlying muscles and organs.
Nervous system	The nervous system of an animal coordinates the activity of the muscles, monitors the organs, constructs and also stops input from the senses, and initiates actions.
Learning	Learning is the acquisition and development of memories and behaviors, including skills, knowledge, understanding, values, and wisdom. It is the goal of education, and the product of experience. Learning ranges from simple forms such as habituation to more complex forms such as play, seen only in large vertebrates.
Classical conditioning	Classical conditioning is a form of associative learning that was first demonstrated by Ivan Pavlov. The typical procedure for inducing classical conditioning involves paired presentations of a neutral stimulus along with a stimulus of some significance. The neutral stimulus could be any event that does not result in an overt behavioral response from the organism under investigation.
Fear conditioning	Fear conditioning is the method by which organisms learn to fear new stimuli. It is a form of learning in which fear is associated with a particular neutral context or neutral stimulus. This can be done by pairing the neutral stimulus with an aversive stimulus. Eventually, the neutral stimulus alone can elicit the state of fear.
Conditioning	Conditioning is a form of associative learning that was first demonstrated by Ivan Pavlov. The typical procedure for inducing classical conditioning involves presentations of a neutral stimulus along with a stimulus of some significance. The neutral stimulus could be any event that does not result in an overt behavioral response from the organism under investigation.

Go to **Cram101.com** for the Practice Tests for this Chapter.
And, **NEVER** highlight a book again!

Operant conditioning	Operant conditioning is the use of consequences to modify the occurrence and form of behavior. It deals with the modification of "voluntary behavior" through the use of consequences. According to the laws of operant conditioning, any behavior that is consistently rewarded, every single time, will extinguish at a faster rate while intermittently reinforcing behavior leads to more stable rates of behavior that are relatively more resistant to extinction.
Observational learning	Observational learning occurs as a function of observing, retaining and replicating behavior observed in others. It is most associated with the work of psychologist Albert Bandura, who implemented some of the seminal studies in the area and initiated social learning theory. It involves the process of learning to copy or model the action of another through observing another doing it.
Exposure effect	Exposure effect is a psychological phenomenon well known to advertisers: people express undue liking for things merely because they are familiar with them. The effect might be explained by the idea that recognizing a familiar environment makes us feel safe.
Arousal	Arousal is a physiological and psychological state involving the activation of the reticular activating system in the brain stem, the autonomic nervous system and the endocrine system, leading to increased heart rate and blood pressure and a condition of alertness and readiness to respond.
Declarative memory	Declarative memory is the aspect of human memory that stores facts. It is so called because it refers to memories that can be consciously discussed, or declared. It applies to standard textbook learning and knowledge, as well memories that can be 'travelled back to' in one's 'mind's eye'.
Memory	In psychology, memory is an organism's ability to store, retain, and subsequently retrieve information. In recent decades, it has become one of the principal pillars of a branch of science called cognitive neuroscience, an interdisciplinary link between cognitive psychology and neuroscience.
Stress	Stress is the disruption of homeostasis through physical or psychological stimuli. Stressful stimuli can be mental, physiological, anatomical or physical reactions. Responses to stress include adaptation, psychological coping such as stress management, anxiety, and depression.
Public	Public is about the what of belonging to the people; relating to, or affecting, a nation, state, or community; opposed to private; as, the public treasury, a road or lake.
Flashbulb memory	A flashbulb memory is a memory that was laid down in great detail during a personally significant event, often a shocking event of national or international importance.
Attention	Attention is the cognitive process of selectively concentrating on one aspect of the environment while ignoring other things. Examples include listening carefully to what someone is saying while ignoring other conversations in the room or listening to a cell phone conversation while driving a car.
Perception	In psychology. and the cognitive sciences, perception is the process of acquiring, interpreting, selecting, and organizing sensory information. It is a task far more complex than was imagined in the 1950s and 1960s, when it was proclaimed that building perceiving machines would take about a decade, but, needless to say, that is still very far from reality.
Attentional blink	Attentional blink is a phenomenon observed in rapid serial visual presentation (RSVP). When presented with a sequence of visual stimuli in rapid succession at the same spatial location on a screen, a participant will often fail to detect a second salient target occurring in succession if it is presented between 200-500ms after the first one.

Go to **Cram101.com** for the Practice Tests for this Chapter.
And, **NEVER** highlight a book again!

Decision	A decision is a final product of a specific mental/cognitive process by an individual or group, which is called decision making, or in more detail, Inactive decision making, Reactive decision making, and Proactive decision making.
Decision making	Decision making is the cognitive process leading to the selection of a course of action among variations. Every decision making process produces a final choice. It can be an action or an opinion. It begins when we need to do something but know not what. Therefore, decision making is a reasoning process which can be rational or irrational, and can be based on explicit assumptions or tacit assumptions.
Science	Science in the broadest sense, refers to any systematic knowledge or practice.[1] In a more restricted sense, science refers to a system of developing explanations for what we observe in the world around us based on the scientific method, as well as to the organized body of such knowledge gained through such research.[2][3] It incorporates the philosophies of naturalism and mechanism and employs reasoning. This article focuses on the more restricted use of the word.
Cognition	In psychology, cognition refers to an information processing view of an individual's psychological functions. Other interpretations of the meaning of cognition link it to the development of concepts; individual minds, groups, organizations, and even larger coalitions of entities, can be modelled as societies which cooperate to form concepts.
Belief	Belief is the psychological state in which an individual is convinced of the truth or validity of a proposition or premise without the ability to adequately prove their main contention for other people who may disagree.
Number	A number is an abstract idea used in counting and measuring. A symbol which represents a number is called a numeral, but in common usage the word number is used for both the idea and the symbol. In addition to their use in counting and measuring, numerals are often used for labels, for ordering, and for codes.
Rationality	Rationality as a term is related to the idea of reason, a word which following Webster's may be derived as much from older terms referring to thinking itself as from giving an account or an explanation. This lends the term a dual aspect. One aspect associates it with comprehension, intelligence, or inference, particularly when an inference is drawn in ordered ways. The other part associates rationality with explanation, understanding or justification, particularly if it provides a ground or a motive.
Risk	Risk is a concept that denotes a potential negative impact to an asset or some characteristic of value that may arise from some present process or future event. In everyday usage, risk is often used synonymously with the probability of a known loss.
Variance	In probability theory and statistics, the variance of a random variable or somewhat more precisely, of a probability distribution is one measure of statistical dispersion, averaging the squared distance of its possible values from the expected value.
Attitude	Attitude is a hypothetical construct that represents an individual's like or dislike for an item. Attitudes are positive, negative or neutral views of an "attitude object": i.e. a person, behavior or event.
Weight	In the physical sciences, weight is a measurement of the gravitational force acting on an object. Near the surface of the Earth, the acceleration due to gravity is approximately constant; this means that an object's weight is roughly proportional to its mass.
Human	Human are bipedal primates in the family Hominidae. Compared to other living organisms on Earth, human s have a highly developed brain capable of abstract reasoning, language, and introspection. This
Theory	In common usage, people often use the word theory to signify a conjecture, an opinion, or a

Go to **Cram101.com** for the Practice Tests for this Chapter.

Go to **Cram101.com** for the Practice Tests for this Chapter.
And, **NEVER** highlight a book again!

speculation. In this usage, a theory is not necessarily based on facts; in other words, it is not required to be consistent with true descriptions of reality.

Emotion	Emotion, in its most general definition, is a complex psychophysical process that arises spontaneously, rather than through conscious effort, and evokes either a positive or negative psychological response and physical expressions, often involuntary, related to feelings, perceptions or beliefs about elements, objects or relations between them, in reality or in the imagination. An emotion is often differentiated from a feeling.
Paradox	A paradox can be an apparently true statement or group of statements that leads to a contradiction or a situation which defies intuition; or it can be, seemingly opposite, an apparent contradiction that actually expresses a non-dual truth.
Role	A role is a set of connected behaviors, rights and obligations as conceptualized by actors in a social situation. It is mostly defined as an expected behavior in a given individual social status and social position.
Judgment	A judgment is synonymous with the formal decision made by a court following a lawsuit. At the same time the court may also make a range of court orders, such as imposing a sentence upon a guilty defendant in a criminal matter, or providing a remedy for the plaintiff in a civil law matter.
Uncertainty	Uncertainty applies to predictions of future events, to physical measurements already made, or to the unknown unknown.
Availability heuristic	The availability heuristic, where people base their prediction of the frequency of an event or the proportion within a population based on how easily an example can be brought to mind. In these instances the ease of imagining an example or the vividness and emotional impact of that example becomes more credible than actual statistical probability.
Bias	A bias is a prejudice in a general or specific sense, usually in the sense for having a preference to one particular point of view or ideological perspective.
Heuristic	A heuristic is a method for helping in solving of a problem, commonly informal. It is particularly used for a method that often rapidly leads to a solution that is usually reasonably close to the best possible answer.
Illusion	An illusion is a distortion of a sensory perception, revealing how the brain normally organizes and interprets sensory stimulation. While illusions distort reality, they are generally shared by most people. Illusions may occur with more of the human senses than vision, but visual illusions, optical illusions, are the most well known and understood.

Problem	A problem is an obstacle which makes it difficult to achieve a desired goal, objective or purpose. It refers to a situation, condition, or issue that is yet unresolved.
Structure	Structure is a fundamental and sometimes intangible notion covering the recognition, observation, nature, and stability of patterns and relationships of entities.
Space	The idea of space has been of interest for philosophers and scientists for much of human history. The term is used somewhat differently in different fields of study, hence it is difficult to provide an uncontroversial and clear definition outside of specific defined
Theory	In common usage, people often use the word theory to signify a conjecture, an opinion, or a speculation. In this usage, a theory is not necessarily based on facts; in other words, it is not required to be consistent with true descriptions of reality.
Heuristic	A heuristic is a method for helping in solving of a problem, commonly informal. It is particularly used for a method that often rapidly leads to a solution that is usually reasonably close to the best possible answer.
Means-ends analysis	Means-Ends Analysis is a technique used in Artificial Intelligence for controlling search in problem solving computer programs. It is also a technique used at least since the 1950s as a creativity tool, most frequently mentioned in engineering books on design methods.
Memory	In psychology, memory is an organism's ability to store, retain, and subsequently retrieve information. In recent decades, it has become one of the principal pillars of a branch of science called cognitive neuroscience, an interdisciplinary link between cognitive psychology and neuroscience.
Problem solving	Problem solving forms part of thinking. Considered the most complex of all intellectual functions, problem solving has been defined as higher-order cognitive process that requires the modulation and control of more routine or fundamental skills.
Role	A role is a set of connected behaviors, rights and obligations as conceptualized by actors in a social situation. It is mostly defined as an expected behavior in a given individual social status and social position.
Working memory	Working memory is a theoretical framework within cognitive psychology that refers to the structures and processes used for temporarily storing and manipulating information. There are numerous theories as to both the theoretical structure of working memory as well as to the specific parts of the brain responsible for working memory.
Functional magnetic resonance imaging	Functional magnetic resonance imaging is the use of MRI to measure the haemodynamic response related to neural activity in the brain or spinal cord of humans or other animals. It is one of the most recently developed forms of neuroimaging.
Goal-oriented	Goal-oriented is a property of systems which are able to think/reason/inference using symbols. A system, person, or organization that tends to achieve a goal and demonstrate it in subsequent actions is said to be goal-oriented.
Expert	An expert is someone widely recognized as a reliable source of technique or skill whose faculty for judging or deciding rightly, justly, or wisely is accorded authority and status by their peers or the public. An expert, more generally, is a person with extensive knowledge or ability in a particular area of study.
Reasoning	Reasoning is the mental process of looking for reasons for beliefs, conclusions, actions or feelings. Humans have the ability to engage in reasoning about their own reasoning using introspection. Different forms of such reflection on reasoning occur in different fields.
Induction	Induction is a method of artificially or prematurely stimulating labor in a woman.

Go to **Cram101.com** for the Practice Tests for this Chapter.
And, **NEVER** highlight a book again!

Strategy	A strategy is a long term plan of action designed to achieve a particular goal, most often "winning".
Inductive reasoning	Inductive reasoning is the process of reasoning in which the premises of an argument are believed to support the conclusion but do not ensure it. It is used to ascribe properties or relations to types based on tokens; or to formulate laws based on limited observations of recurring phenomenal patterns.
Wisconsin Card Sorting Test	The Wisconsin Card Sorting Test is a neuropsychological test of "set-shifting", i.e. the ability to display flexibility in the face of changing schedules of reinforcement.
Brain	In animals, the brain, is the control center of the central nervous system, responsible for behavior. The brain is located in the head, protected by the skull and close to the primary sensory apparatus of vision, hearing, equilibrioception, sense of acceleration, taste, and olfaction.
PET	A pet is an animal kept for companionship and enjoyment, as opposed to livestock, laboratory animals, working animals or sport animals, which are kept for economic reasons.
Deductive reasoning	Deductive reasoning is the kind of reasoning where the conclusion is necessitated by previously known premises. If the premises are true then the conclusion must be true.
Syllogism	A syllogism is a kind of logical argument in which one proposition is inferred from two others of a certain form. The syllogism is at the core of deductive reasoning, where facts are determined by combining existing statements, in contrast to inductive reasoning where facts are determined by repeated observations.
Wason selection task	the Wason selection task is a logic puzzle which is formally equivalent to the following question: You are shown a set of four cards placed on a table each of which has a number on one side and a colored patch on the other side. The visible faces of the cards show 3, 8, red and brown. Which cards should you turn over in order to test the truth of the proposition that if a card shows an even number on one face, then its opposite face shows a primary
Logic	Logic is the study of the principles and criteria of valid inference and demonstration.
Mind	Mind collectively refers to the aspects of intellect and consciousness manifested as combinations of thought, perception, memory, emotion, will and imagination; mind is the stream of consciousness.

Go to **Cram101.com** for the Practice Tests for this Chapter.
And, **NEVER** highlight a book again!

Cognition	In psychology, cognition refers to an information processing view of an individual's psychological functions. Other interpretations of the meaning of cognition link it to the development of concepts; individual minds, groups, organizations, and even larger coalitions
Supplementary motor area	The supplementary motor area is a part of the sensorimotor cerebral cortex. It was included, on purely cytoarchitectonic arguments, in area 6 of Brodmann and the Vogts. It is located on the medial face of the hemisphere, just in front of the primary motor cortex. This is an element that appeared late in evolution, in monkeys, linked to the appearance of a true medial pallidum.
Brain	In animals, the brain, is the control center of the central nervous system, responsible for behavior. The brain is located in the head, protected by the skull and close to the primary sensory apparatus of vision, hearing, equilibrioception, sense of acceleration, taste, and olfaction.
Role	A role is a set of connected behaviors, rights and obligations as conceptualized by actors in a social situation. It is mostly defined as an expected behavior in a given individual social status and social position.
Mind	Mind collectively refers to the aspects of intellect and consciousness manifested as combinations of thought, perception, memory, emotion, will and imagination; mind is the stream of consciousness.
Priming	Priming in psychology refers to activating parts of particular representations or associations in memory just before carrying out an action or task. It is considered to be one of the manifestations of implicit memory. A property of priming is that the remembered item is remembered best in the form in which it was originally encountered. If a priming list is given in an auditory mode, then an auditory cue produces better performance than a visual
Research	Research is a human activity based on intellectual investigation and aimed at discovering, interpreting, and revising human knowledge on different aspects of the world. Research can use the scientific method, but need not do so.
Power	Much of the recent sociological debate on power revolves around the issue of the enabling nature of power.
Perspective	Perspective in theory of cognition is the choice of a context or a reference or the result of this choice from which to sense, categorize, measure or codify experience, cohesively forming a coherent belief, typically for comparing with another
Mental rotation	Mental rotation is the ability to rotate mental representations of two-dimensional and three-dimensional objects. It usually takes place in the right cerebral hemisphere, in the areas where perception also occurs. It is associated with the rate of spatial processing and intelligence.
Intention	Intention is performing an action is their specific purpose in doing so, the end or goal they aim at, or intend to accomplish.
Observation	Observation is an activity of a sapient or sentient living being, which senses and assimilates the knowledge of a phenomenon in its framework of previous knowledge and ideas.
Apraxia	Apraxia is a neurological disorder characterized by loss of the ability to execute or carry out learned movements, despite having the desire and the physical ability to perform the movements.
Imitation	Imitation is an advanced behavior whereby an individual observes and replicates another's. The word can be applied in many contexts, ranging from animal training to international politics.
Understanding	Understanding is a psychological process related to an abstract or physical object, such as,

Go to **Cram101.com** for the Practice Tests for this Chapter.

Go to Cram101.com for the Practice Tests for this Chapter.
And, NEVER highlight a book again!

person, situation, or message whereby one is able to think about it and use concepts to deal adequately with that object.

Mirror neuron	A mirror neuron is a neuron which fires both when an animal acts and when the animal observes the same action performed by another animal. In humans, brain activity consistent with mirror neurons has been found in the premotor cortex and the inferior parietal cortex. It has the potential to provide a mechanism for action understanding, imitation learning, and the simulation of other people's behavior.
Neuron	The neuron is the primary cell of the nervous system. They are found in the brain, the spinal cord, in the nerves and ganglia of the peripheral nervous system. It is a specialized cell that conducts impulses through the nervous system and contains three major parts: cell body, dendrites, and an axon. It can have many dendrites but only one axon.
Theory	In common usage, people often use the word theory to signify a conjecture, an opinion, or a speculation. In this usage, a theory is not necessarily based on facts; in other words, it is not required to be consistent with true descriptions of reality.
Transcranial magnetic stimulation	A Transcranial magnetic stimulation is a noninvasive method to excite neurons in the brain.
Stimulation	Stimulation is the action of various agents on muscles, nerves, or a sensory end organ, by which activity is evoked.
Biology	Biology is the scientific study of life. Biology examines the structure, function, growth, origin, evolution, and distribution of living things.
Perception	In psychology. and the cognitive sciences, perception is the process of acquiring, interpreting, selecting, and organizing sensory information. It is a task far more complex than was imagined in the 1950s and 1960s, when it was proclaimed that building perceiving machines would take about a decade, but, needless to say, that is still very far from reality.
Motion perception	Motion perception is the process of inferring the speed and direction of objects and surfaces that move in a visual scene given some visual input. Although this process appears straightforward to most observers, it has proven to be a difficult problem from a computational perspective, and extraordinarily difficult to explain in terms of neural processing.
Asynchrony	Asynchrony, in the general meaning, is the state of not being synchronized. In specific terms of digital logic and physical layer of communication, an asynchronous process does not require a clock signal.
Locomotion	In biomechanics, locomotion is the study of how animals move. Locomotive ability is widespread throughout the animal kingdom. As all animals are heterotrophs, they must obtain food from their environment. Most animals must move around to find food, a mate, and so forth. Ability to do so efficiently is therefore essential to their survival.

Go to **Cram101.com** for the Practice Tests for this Chapter.
And, **NEVER** highlight a book again!

Animal language	Animal language is the modeling of human language in non human animal systems.
Language	A language is a system of symbols and the rules used to manipulate them. Language can also refer to the use of such systems as a general phenomenon. Though commonly used as a means of communication among people, human language is only one instance of this phenomenon.
Syntax	In linguistics, syntax are the rules of a language that show how the words of that language are to be arranged to make a sentence of that language. The term syntax can also be used to refer to these rules themselves, as in "the syntax of Gaelic". Modern research in syntax attempts to describe languages in terms of such rules, and, for many practitioners, to find general rules that apply to all languages. Since the field of syntax attempts to explain
Brain	In animals, the brain, is the control center of the central nervous system, responsible for behavior. The brain is located in the head, protected by the skull and close to the primary sensory apparatus of vision, hearing, equilibrioception, sense of acceleration, taste, and olfaction.
Broca face=symbol>-s area	Broca's area is a section of the human brain that is involved in language processing, speech production and comprehension.
Sign Language	A sign language is a language which uses manual communication, body language and lip patterns instead of sound to convey meaning—simultaneously combining hand shapes, orientation and movement of the hands, arms or body, and facial expressions to express fluidly a speaker's thoughts. Sign languages commonly develop in deaf communities, which can include interpreters and friends and families of deaf people as well as people who are deaf or hard of hearing themselves.
Phoneme	In human language, a phoneme is the smallest structural unit that distinguishes meaning. They are not the physical segments themselves, but, in theoretical terms, cognitive abstractions of them.
Animal	An animal is part of a major group of multicellular organisms, of the kingdom Animalia or Metazoa. Their body plan becomes fixed as they develop, usually early on in their development as embryos, although some undergo a process of metamorphosis later on in their life.
Communication	Communication is a process that allows organisms to exchange information by several methods. Communication requires that all parties understand a common language that is exchanged. There are auditory means, such as speaking,singing and sometimes tone of voice, and nonverbal, physical means, such as body language, sign language, paralanguage, touch, eye contact, or the use of writing.
Speech	Speech refers to the processes associated with the production and perception of sounds used in spoken language. A number of academic disciplines study speech and speech sounds, including acoustics, psychology, speech pathology, linguistics, and computer science.
Speech perception	Speech perception refers to the processes by which humans are able to interpret and understand the sounds used in language. The study of speech perception is closely linked to the fields of phonetics and phonology in linguistics and cognitive psychology and perception in psychology. Research in speech perception seeks to understand how human listeners recognize speech sounds and use this information to understand spoken language.
Comprehension	The comprehension of an object is the totality of intensions, that is, attributes, characters, marks, properties, or qualities, that the object possesses, or else the totality of intensions that are pertinent to the context of a given discussion. This is the correct technical term for the whole collection of intensions of an object.
Lexicon	In linguistics, the lexicon of a language is its vocabulary, including its words and expressions. More formally, it is a language's inventory of lexemes.

Go to **Cram101.com** for the Practice Tests for this Chapter.

Go to **Cram101.com** for the Practice Tests for this Chapter.
And, **NEVER** highlight a book again!

Perception	In psychology. and the cognitive sciences, perception is the process of acquiring, interpreting, selecting, and organizing sensory information. It is a task far more complex than was imagined in the 1950s and 1960s, when it was proclaimed that building perceiving machines would take about a decade, but, needless to say, that is still very far from reality.
Bottom-up	If your attention is drawn to a flower in a field, it may be simply that the flower is more visually salient than the surrounding field. The information which caused you to attend to the flower came to you in a bottom-up fashion -- your attention was not contingent upon knowledge of the flower; the outside stimulus was sufficient on its own.
Top-down	Top-down processing is the observation that person's perception and recognition of objects is influenced by the physical and mental context in which the objects are encountered.
Identification	Identification is a term that is used in different meanings in psychoanalysis. The roots of the concept can be found in Freud's writings. Freud established five concepts of identification of which the three most important concepts will be discussed below. We finalise with the current concept of identification as is mostly seen in psychoanalytic thinking today.
Problem	A problem is an obstacle which makes it difficult to achieve a desired goal, objective or purpose. It refers to a situation, condition, or issue that is yet unresolved.
Hypothesis	A hypothesis consists either of a suggested explanation for a phenomenon or of a reasoned proposal suggesting a possible correlation between multiple phenomena.
Cohort	A cohort is a group of individuals defined by their date of birth. Some cohort studies track a group of children from their birth, and record a wide range of information about them. The value of a cohort depends on the researchers' capacity to stay in touch with all members of the cohort.
Reading	Reading is the cognitive process of deriving meaning from written or printed text.
Encoding	Encoding (in cognition) is a basic perceptual process of interpreting incoming stimuli; technically speaking, it is a complex, multi-stage process of converting relatively objective sensory input (e.g., light, sound) into subjectively meaningful experience.
Structure	Structure is a fundamental and sometimes intangible notion covering the recognition, observation, nature, and stability of patterns and relationships of entities.
Nominal aphasia	Nominal aphasia is a form of aphasia in which the subject has difficulty remembering or recognizing names which the subject should know well. The subject speaks fluently and grammatically, and has normal comprehension; the only deficit is trouble with "word finding," that is, finding appropriate words for what they mean to say.
Thought	Thought is a mental process that allows beings to model the world and to deal with it effectively according to their goals, plans, ends and desires.
Multilingualism	The term multilingualism can refer to phenomena regarding an individual speaker who uses two or more languages, a community of speakers where two or more languages are used, or between speakers of different languages.
Menstruation	Menstruation is a phase of the menstrual cycle in which the uterine lining is shed. Menstrual cycles occur exclusively in humans and other apes.

Go to **Cram101.com** for the Practice Tests for this Chapter.

Go to **Cram101.com** for the Practice Tests for this Chapter.
And, **NEVER** highlight a book again!

Lightning Source UK Ltd.
Milton Keynes UK
UKOW01f0026071014

239730UK00005B/302/P

9 781428 859722